The Laws of Impartation

By

PHILLIP RICH

EKKLISIA PROPHETIC APOSTOLIC MINISTRIES, INC.

Published By Ekklisia Ministries

Take note that the name satan is not capitalized. We choose not to acknowledge him, even to the point of violating grammatical rules

TABLE OF CONTENTS

ACKNOWLEDGEMENT

The information in this book came about because of a deep hunger to be used by God in a greater measure. In my search for understanding the Lord revealed it to me through His Word and through seasoned ministers who carry His anointing and power.

Special thanks is given to my wife, Connie, whose prayers and support have kept me going all these years. And to my children, Kisha, Stan, Rachel, Ryan, Chris, and Amber.

I want to also thank my father Lee Rich who was my first mentor, he taught me to love God and my family and whose exemplary lifestyle of constant dedication to Jesus has helped guide me even to this day. My Spirit rejoices in knowing that he is worshipping around the throne of God and will one day welcome me there. And to my Mother, Dorothy Wall, and my step Dad, Harold Wall, who both pray for me non-stop day by day.

Acknowledgment is also given to Dr. Mike Brown of Strength and Wisdom Ministries, whose revelation of honor and wisdom has helped encourage and exemplify the teaching that is in this book. And also to my late Apostle Fred Pine of King's Business Ministries who imparted many wonderful thing into my life which I will be eternally grateful.

And, of course, a special thanks to our prayer partners and supporters whose names are in the Lamb's Book of Life. May God reward you richly for your labor of love toward us.

Impart

GK - metadidomi

To give over- to share based on connection and association.

FORWARD

Many believers know the King, but they do not know the King's Laws. Knowing the King makes us ready for Heaven, however knowing the King's Laws makes us successful on the earth. When God wants to bring new wisdom or anointing, He brings a person with something in them to impart to another. Moses imparted to Joshua, Elijah imparted to Elijah, Paul imparted to Timothy.

In his book, Prophet Phil Rich will lead you on a journey of revelation concerning receiving the impartation of anointing you need to fulfill your life's assignment. The knowledge you receive in this book will promote you in God's Kingdom and bring you into new areas of influence for His glory!

Dr. Mike Brown

Romans 1:11 For I long to see you, that I may impart unto you some spiritual gift, to the end ye may be established;

INTRODUCTION

God has given the five-fold ministry to the church to impart to Christians that which we don't have yet, but which is available. In God everything is available. In Him we live, move and have our being. We have everything we need in life and godliness through the knowledge of Him.[1]

Philippians 4:9; *"Those things, which ye have both learned, and received, and heard, and seen in me, do: and the God of peace shall be with you."*

Paul wrote this to the church at Philippi, a church that had become a covenant partner with him in the work of the Lord. They joined with him.

In chapter 1, Paul said he thanked God in every remembrance of them. He must have had some good memories if he thanked God every time he thought about them. He must have seen some good things happen in that body of believers when he was there.

Philippians 1:3-5; *"I thank my God upon every remembrance of you, Always in every prayer of mine for you all making request with joy, For your fellowship in the gospel from the first day until now"*

Fellowship means koinonia or partnership.

Philippians 1:6; *"Being confident of this very thing, that he which hath begun a good work in you will perform it until the day of Jesus Christ:"*

Paul had raised up this church in Philippi. He told them he was very confident that the work God had started in them, through his ministry, He would complete. God would perform it until the day of Jesus Christ. It would keep happening, until they came into the perfection that was available for them.

---

[1] 2 Peter 1:3

Philippians 1:7; ***"Even as it is meet for me to think this of you all, because I have you in my heart; inasmuch as both in my bonds, and in the defence and confirmation of the gospel, ye all are partakers of my grace."***

A lot of people see covenant as bondage, as being locked in, controlled by something, held into something. Covenant is actually a connection that enables you to have everything that the person you are connecting to has. In reality, covenant gives you access to anointings and abilities that you don't have. It gives you more than you had before. Covenant is not a place of limitation, but of increase. If you come into a godly covenant, there are no strings attached in the natural. It is a heart-to-heart thing. That is why Paul could say that he had them in his heart.

There can't be impartation without covenant relationship. In fact, the first law of impartation is covenant relation. You have to connect with somebody who has something you don't have.

No one person has it all. The bible says we all have gifts differing. Each one has a measure of faith. It doesn't say that one person has all the faith.[2] A measure doesn't mean the whole thing. You have a certain amount of faith and I have a certain amount of faith. When we join hands together in a covenant relationship, I not only have my faith but I have your faith also. You not only have your faith but you have my faith. You have doubled your faith just by understanding that somebody else has something you don't have.

When it comes to understanding the laws of impartation, we have to walk in humility and not pride. If we think we have it all, then we are not going to want to connect with anybody to get impartation. It's sad, but there are also ministries with that attitude. They have limited themselves to that which only they have and there is no more. They can never operate in corporate anointing because they are too locked into individual anointing. They will never operate in corporate glory, corporate faith, or corporate anointing. All they will ever have is their individual measure, which is not very much because they have limited themselves.

---

[2] Romans 12:3

God does not want us to have limitation, but unlimited ability, and we can. We must understand that God has a body, His people, and He has invested in each one a particular measure of faith and anointings.

1 John 2:27a; ***"But the anointing which ye have received"***

So, each one of us has only a measure of an anointing. But, as soon as we come into covenant with another, then we not only have the anointing we have, but we also have the anointing of the person we are in covenant with. So, we have already doubled, tripled or quadrupled our anointing. It is through connection that we become more than we are.

I get what all the ministries I am connected with have. So, when I minister I can draw on all of those different anointings along with the anointing I have in my own life. I can operate in all of those and move in a vein where there is not the limitation there would be if I were going to operate only in what I have.

So, we see that there has to be relationship and association. You have to have a covenant relationship. We see this demonstrated in 1 Kings 19, with Elisha and Elijah. Elijah came along because he was told by God to go and anoint Elisha in his room, in his place. He was to anoint Elisha to live in the same anointings he lived in.

There was an invitation before there was a relation. The invitation came with Elijah coming and throwing his mantle around Elisha. He gave Elisha the opportunity to feel the anointing, to taste a little of it and then he left, walked out of the village.

That left Elisha with a decision to be made. God will let you taste a ministry, but you have to do something with it. Ministries will come along and throw a mantle over you, let you feel some things, let you hear some things, let you experience some things and then they will walk on. I can't force you to be a covenant partner with me. I can't force you to be a part of our ministry. I can only come along and minister to you. You will feel the mantle. But then I have to walk on and you have to decide that you are going after it, because you want to be a part of it.

I am not supposed to be chasing you. You are supposed to be chasing me. That means if God brings a ministry to lay an anointing on you so you feel some of it, then you have to make the decision whether or not you want to be part of it.

When Elisha made that decision, he first wanted to take care of some other things. Elijah asked what that had to do with him. In other words, if Elisha didn't want to follow Elijah that was fine. It was up to Elisha. He knew Elisha had things to do, bills to pay, his own life, but who doesn't.

You can come or not come to the meeting. You can give or not give in the offering. It is up to you. If you will be a part, you will get a part, but you have to connect.

And so Elisha ran after Elijah. Never once did scripture say that the prophet had to chase Elisha around and remind him of everything. No, if you can't perceive, you can't receive.

Elisha had a destiny, but that destiny could not be realized without understanding there had to be an impartation from a man of God who had something to give. Elisha had to perceive it in order to receive it. He had to go after, run after the man of God and position himself in order to get everything Elijah had.

Many people today are not positioning themselves. They are going to get their prophecy, to get ministered to. They won't see that minister again until they have a need and so will never get an impartation. They will come to get ministered to so that they can get out of that moment of trouble, not realizing they will never see their destiny fulfilled.

Saul went to see the prophet to find out about his missing donkeys.[3] A lot of people are worried about their donkeys and will go to see the prophet. But the prophet has a lot more to give than a word about donkeys, about fixing the momentary problem. He can impart and train to bring you into your destiny, but you have to connect with him.

---

[3] 1 Samuel 9

You have to connect to your Pastor to get an impartation from him. Do you only go to the Pastor when you have a need? Some people do. But you don't get the impartation that way. You need to sit under that pastor on a regular basis and connect with him.

You need to connect with the teacher, the evangelist, the prophet and the apostle. You have to realize it is a covenant relationship that will bring impartation into your life.

Elisha rose, went after Elijah and ministered to him. *"Ministered unto"* means to contribute, to help, to assist. It refers to contributions, finances, encouragement, anything you can do that will help the man of God.

Let's look at how people ministered to Jesus.

Luke 8:1-3; ***"And it came to pass afterward, that he went throughout every city and village, preaching and shewing the glad tidings of the kingdom of God: and the twelve were with him, And certain women, which had been healed of evil spirits and infirmities, Mary called Magdalene, out of whom went seven devils, And Joanna the wife of Chuza Herod's steward, and Susanna, and many others, which ministered unto him of their substance."***

These women had felt the mantle of Jesus and had been healed of evil spirits and infirmities. They ministered to Jesus by supporting him with material goods, not by prophesying to Him or giving Him good words.

I prophesy to people to give them impartations so they can prophesy, so that they can hear God better and to confirm to them what they have already heard so that they know they can hear God.

I don't need you to do that for me. If I did, I would have no right to stand in front of a group of people. I know how to hear the Lord. I have been trained, been imparted to, had prophets and apostles prophesy to me and minister to me for years. Many times people want to minister to the minister and they want to do it by giving him a prophecy. They want to lay hands on the minister and help him somehow.

I have apostles and prophets over me who minister to me on a regular basis. There is a chain of command. The five-fold ministry can minister to the five-fold ministry in a way different than just ministers can. If I am training you, then I don't need to hear God through you.

In an army can you imagine a private going to the commanding officer under the President and giving him a word? It won't happen. It is not because the private is not important, but because there is a chain of command. There are levels of authority. Authority warrants a certain amount of respect. The way you minister to those in authority over you is out of your substance. We saw that in Luke 8:1-3. If they had come to Jesus with a prophecy it would have been out of order. If they had come to Jesus and said they wanted to lay hands on Him and impart some things to Him, it would have been out of order. So, how did they minister to Him? They gave the substance that was needed.

Paul said it this way, "*If I give unto you that which is spiritual, it is only right that you give unto me that which is natural.*"[4] He didn't say that if he gave them spiritually they should give him spiritually. You cannot run a ministry if the only way people are going to give back to you is spiritual. Telling someone to be clothed or be fed without giving them clothing or food will not meet their need.

It is important for you to pray for me, but if you think that is the only way you are going to minister to me, you are missing something. They ministered to Jesus out of their substance.

It is called the laws of impartation. If we understand these things we will understand how it works. If a ministry blesses you, connects to you and you realize they have something, you need to become a partner with them.

The church at Philippi gave once and again unto his necessity.[5] They were constantly sending what he needed. That is how they partnered

---

[4] 1 Corinthians 9:11
[5] Philippians 4:16

with him. Ministries need you to pray for them and financially support them. They need for you to connect with them and be in their services.

Have you ever had something wonderful and couldn't share it with anyone? It is like filling up on the things that God wants you to feed somebody and there is nobody to take it from you. When I was growing up we had a cow that gave birth to a calf that died. The cow had milk for the calf but had no way of giving it out. She was in pain because there was no calf to draw out the nourishment. Those in the five-fold ministry fill up on the things of God and there is nobody to draw it out. When people come to a meeting hungry there is a flowing out of the minister the things that God has given them. That brings an amazing fulfillment for the minister.

You are not anointed because you hear God. You are anointed because you obey what you heard.

THE IMPORTANCE OF IMPARTATIONS

God wants us to understand how to tap into the grace, anointings, ministries that others have because everything that is flowing through the ministry to supposed to go to the people. When you connect with a ministry, the mantle, gifts and anointing they have are for you, not for them. They are supposed to get them into your life. God put those things into their life so that they could transfer them to you. A minister is a trainer, an activator and an imparter. That is his job.

The prophets of today are not like the Old Testament prophets who were not imparters to anyone except another prophet. They passed what they had on to the next generation of prophets. New Testament prophets, however, are equippers. Pastors, apostles, teachers and evangelists are all equippers.

Ephesians 4:11-12; "*And he gave some, apostles; and some, prophets; and some, evangelists; and some, pastors and teachers; For the perfecting of the saints, for the work of the ministry, for the edifying of the body of Christ*:"

"For the perfecting of the saints" means to fully furnish the saints with anointings, mantles, impartations and windows into their destinies that are necessary for them to be successful and powerful in the Spirit of the Lord.

When you see a ministry flowing in power and you are in covenant with them, that power is yours. You are looking at yourself in the mirror. That is how you are going to minister. That is what you are supposed to get, but you have to set your faith on it. Some don't know that. "*Well that is just the prophet. That is his gifting. That is how he ministers. Boy, I wish I could.*" You are meant to. It is supposed to be imparted to you.

God is raising up the body of Christ to be powerful, able ministers of the New Covenant who take Jesus to a lost and dying world. That is what it is all about. The five-fold is to impart all of these giftings, all of these anointings, all of these abilities into the body of Christ. The body of Christ then rises up as a powerful army going into all the world and changing the world by the power of Christ.

The five-fold ministry is not composed of great awesome people who are untouchables. They are servants imparting. They are trainers and equippers with things to deliver and they are going to deliver it. They are looking for someone who will connect with them because you have to connect in order to get it.

Covenant Relationships

The Lord is talking more and more about covenant relationships.[6] You can't get what someone else has spiritually without covenant relationships. God will connect everybody with a pastor, with an apostle, with an evangelist, with a prophet, and with a teacher. God will connect everyone with the five-fold. You won't connect with every prophet, every evangelist, every pastor, every teacher, every apostle and you are not supposed to. You might enjoy the ministry of several of them, but you won't connect with every one of them. We are talking about covenant relationships where our heart is knit to the ministry like David and Jonathan's hearts were knit.

The things we receive are received through covenant relationships. What happens in a marriage and what is received in it is because of a covenant relationship. If done in the right way, then in the eyes of God that covenant relationship is a beautiful thing and it works. In the spirit, the same thing is true. You will end up with something demonic if you try to get something illegally in the spirit. With God, you are going to have to do His will His way before it works for you. His way is covenant relationship. You have to connect with those to whom God connects you and join with them, knit your heart to them. Receive what God is pouring through them. What they preach and teach is only one part of it. There is something from their spirit, from their heart that is transferred. The faith they have, the way they move in God, the divine ability and the sensitivity

[6] We have a book available called "Mantles of Authority/Covenant Connections" that deals more in depth with covenant relationships.

they move in is released into your spirit if you receive it and if you know how to connect to it.

Someone who is not in covenant relationship with me will come into my meetings, receive something and I will minister to them. They will be blessed for the moment. But they won't really get a download of what is in my spirit (divine abilities) until there is a covenant relationship made. It takes time to develop the relationship.

I see and connect on a regular basis with other ministries I am in relationship with. I put forth the effort to make the connection. I don't wait for them to make the effort to make a connection with me. The download of divine enablement takes place when I put forth the effort to make the connection. Then, there is something transferred in the realm of the spirit.

You make that connection to get a download, to be equipped, to be furnished, and to have a release of what God has put into the spirit of the minister. It is a tangible mantle of anointings and ability. Not just feeling, but reality. All of a sudden you have divine abilities that you didn't have before. Abilities to hear God in a particular way, to move out into particular things, to see things in a particular way, to perceive things you never perceived before, to move in things you never moved in before and have God move on you in ways He has never moved on you before.

The things I have, I didn't get by myself. It took covenant relationships to get them. There are ministries I have been connected to, from whom I learned how to get the downloads and to make the connection. I learned how to receive the impartations. I learned how to connect with these ministries.

I didn't get it in one service. I didn't get it in two services. In some instances I didn't get it the first year or the second year. It took me three solid years of drawing from one ministry before the download came. Some ministries I will be connected with for the rest of my life before I even begin to get all the download that is there. It is an ongoing thing because those ministries are still getting downloads. I can never get caught up with it and feel like I have it all. There is a constant impartation and a constant transferring being released into my life and ministry so that I can move in things I have never moved in before.

Years ago I had dreams of big things, but I didn't have the substance to produce them. I had big vision, but I didn't have the downloads from the ministries who had the substance that would enable me to fulfill my dream and my vision. If your dream, your vision is not realized yet, you don't fully have all the downloads that you need. If you had all the downloads and all the substance it would already be happening. If it is not, then you still have need of some downloads, some impartations, some things being released and you have to go after them.

Think about Elisha and the first time he felt the mantle of Elijah come around his shoulders. He felt the prophetic power and fire that was in the mantle. No doubt, it was like electrical bolts going through his whole being and he thought, "*I have to get some of that.*" The Bible says he got up and followed Elijah. Then Elisha looked back and realized he had a lot more things he needed to get done first. Elijah said, "*What is that to me? I am going. You do what you want to do. Do you want this or not? I am going on my way.*"

In my ministry, God sends me where I am supposed to be, but I am not chasing people around. They can come into the services and feel the power of it. They can decide if they are going after it or not.

You have to decide if you are going after it or not when you feel the power of God, receive the Word, receive the prophecy, receive the healing, when the presence of God hits you. Do you want that same anointing or not? It is totally up to you. It has nothing to do with me. "*I am not hanging around waiting on you. If you want it let's go. If you don't, I am going somewhere else.*" It is your decision.

Some will say that you are chasing a man. No, you are chasing a mantle, chasing an impartation, chasing your future, chasing your vision, chasing your dream. Elisha was not chasing Elijah around just as a man because he could preach real good. I can tell you that Elijah was not a fun person to hang out with. He would get angry, call down fire and kill people. I'm sure Elisha didn't enjoy Elijah's company but he wasn't after his company. He wasn't after the man. He wasn't looking at the man. He was looking at the ministry, the mantle, the download, the impartation, the substance that was about to be his.

There is no good thing in the flesh. There is nothing in my flesh that you need. The flesh cannot save you, deliver you, or do anything to help you get into your destiny. Too many times we look at the flesh of an individual when the anointing is on them and it looks nice and attractive. But when the anointing is not on them and you see them in the flesh, you may not like them at all. It is not about flesh. We have to look beyond the natural and see the supernatural.

Being led by the Spirit means being in step with the Holy Ghost, being sensitive enough to find out where He is moving and move with Him. If He says to do something, you do it. If He shows you something, you flow with it. If He speaks something to you, you speak it. Whatever He is doing, you are in the flow with Him. You are in a miracle flow and it has nothing to do with you.

Those sensitivities, those anointings, those mantles that enable you to be in sync with Him can be imparted. The ability to see something and be able to perceive it correctly can be imparted. "*But I never hear or see anything you may say.*" Then you need a download. Even if you have had a few downloads you need a lot more. I am after more all the time. I am constantly hungering for more.

Do you have a vision bigger than you on the inside, a dream that cannot be realized by your flesh? Is it so huge that it will take God and a bunch of miracles to bring it to pass? How many downloads are you going to need to see that accomplished? Maybe hundreds, maybe thousands, maybe millions. Who knows how many? But, if it has not been accomplished, then you do not have enough downloads, impartations, or equipment from other ministries.

Some are operating in an anointing or in a mantle, but cannot tell you how to do it. One young man went to a prophetess and asked her, "*How can I begin to hear God? How do you hear God?*" She told him that she didn't know how to tell him. She just knew that she could hear God. She was being honest because she didn't have the anointing or the mantle to share or to impart it. She had impartations in other areas that were very powerful and she could release them, but not that one particular thing. She didn't know how to release what he wanted.

He came to me and asked me the same question. I opened up the Word and began to teach him. I laid it out for him because I have the mantle of teacher and imparter in that area.

We do not all have the same impartations. Each one of us have something different to give and that is why we need each other. That is why the five-fold also need each other. I am not all the five-fold wrapped up in one. Only Jesus is that. Even though I operate in the apostolic and the prophetic, that still does not enable me to operate in all five offices. I can operate in all five different anointings because an apostle can move into these gifts and anointings. But again, that doesn't mean that I occupy each one of those offices in full potential.

No one person has all the mantles, all the anointings, or all the abilities. They may claim to, but they don't. It would be dangerous if they did because they could easily move into pride and destroy lives, including their own. The Lord did not invest them in any one individual. Instead He poured them into the corporate ministry so that we have to rely on each other, draw on one another's anointing, receive downloads and impartations from each other.

"*Well, I have all the gifts of the Holy Spirit.*" Really? What you have is the Holy Spirit who has all nine gifts. As He wills it, you can flow in those gifts. But don't get lifted up in pride, saying you have this and you have that because what you have is the Holy Ghost. The real gifting you have is the gift of the Holy Ghost and the gift of salvation. Repent, be baptized and you shall receive the gift of the Holy Ghost.[7] If you really begin to look at 1 Corinthians 12:1 in the King James Version, you will see that the word "*gifts*" is in italics. It was added by the translators and is not in the original text.

1 Corinthians 12:1; ***"Now concerning spiritual*** [spiritual anointings, spiritual endowments, or the ability to be spiritual] ***<u>gifts</u>*** [things]***, brethren, I would not have you ignorant."***

In the rest of the chapter we need to begin to look at what it is saying when it says gifts. What we call the nine gifts of the Spirit are not

[7] Acts 2:38

really gifts. They are nine manifestations of the Spirit. Those manifestations are given to every man to profit withal.[8] In other words, they are available. You have the Holy Ghost and all nine manifestations are in Him. As He wills it, as He moves and you move in sync with Him, you move in those manifestations. If I possess them then I can operate in them at any time I want. But I don't possess them. What I possess is the Holy Ghost and He possesses me.

Let's say I go into a church where everybody is healed, where nobody is sick. If I say that I possess the gift of healing and try to get something to work, it won't happen because there is not a need for healing, The Holy Spirit is not going to be moving in that direction.

I have to move in sync with the Holy Spirit who will move according to what the need is and what the faith level is. I have to be sensitive enough to the Spirit of God and the needs of the people that I can sense where He is moving, where the people are and where He is. I will begin to move where the Holy Ghost is moving and be in step with Him. If He is moving to bring healing to somebody, then I want to move in that with Him and yield my vessel to flow with Him in the gifts of healings. I am going to listen to what the Holy Spirit tells me as He shows me an illness, a problem or what that person is going through. Then He will have me speak it out in order to get that person's faith connected with me so that together we can release this gift of healing.

The most advantageous way to move in these manifestations is to connect with the hearts of others. If it is only my faith doing it, you won't keep what you just received. I have seen deaf people, who were ministered to and God opened their ears, lose their healing by the time they got out to the parking lot. They were stone-deaf again because it was only my faith and not theirs. In the service they could hear a whisper even when you were walking behind them.

I love words of knowledge because they help me draw on your faith. If the Holy Spirit can give me a word of knowledge about you and you will connect your faith with me through that word of knowledge, then we can see a transfer of one of those manifestations of the Spirit. You will

---

[8] 1Cointhians 12:7

walk out of that service and be able to keep what you just received. This is why I prefer moving by revelation.

There are four different ways to move in healing. I can share the Word of God with you and you take the Word, believe it and receive it. I can lay hands on you and release a healing flow. I can give a word of knowledge that you connect with by your faith and healing is released. The last way is the prayer of agreement.

Prophets move more by revelation than any other way. I will still preach the Word, will still lay hands on people but I prefer the vocal way of giving a word of knowledge by the Holy Spirit showing me something. When I get a word of knowledge it causes the gift of faith to kick in inside of me. I know that I know that I know you are about to receive a miracle. It is impossible for it not to happen.

With the prayer of agreement, I don't always know that I know that I know. If you walk up to me, tell me you have a need and ask me to pray with you, I will do it, but I can't tell you the gift of faith is there. I can't stir that up. People want to run to the prophet, tell him all their needs, their problems and then expect the prophet to still operate in a high level of power. It won't work. I have to operate by revelatory anointing. Then the gift of faith will kick in and there will be the working of miracles.

<u>If you will accommodate the Holy Spirit, He will accompany you.</u> He will not accommodate you. Remember the dove that Noah turned loose from the ark? It went out searching for a place. In other words, it went out on a visitation looking for a habitation. It couldn't find a resting place so it returned. When it was sent out again it returned with an olive leaf. That meant there was life out there, but it still was not a habitation. The third time the dove found habitation and did not return to the ark.[9]

The dove is a type of the Holy Spirit. He will move in our lives in a visitation, but don't mistake visitation for a habitation. Just because He visits you doesn't mean He is going to stay. He will go through your house to see if everything He wants is there.

---

[9] Genesis 8:8-12

A lot of churches have a revival week once a year. They expect God to move that one week and He may, but the week after revival it is a dead church again. They thought that the visitation was a habitation. However, the Holy Ghost was only checking it out. The Spirit of the Lord came in and tried to find a place to rest. He stayed a week. Was there a heart that was tender? Was there anyone who would pray on a regular basis? Was there anyone who would do what He wanted, anyone who would lay their life down and be selfless instead of selfish, anyone He could do a work in? If He can't find anyone, He will leave. Those churches get all upset because they don't know what happened. They were having a wonderful time for that week and now their church is dead again.

In the natural, you will visit an apartment you are going to rent or the house you are looking to buy. Visiting it doesn't mean you are going to live there. When you visit it, you walk through every room and check it out to see if it would be accommodating for you and if it would have everything you need to be comfortable living there. Your visitation does not mean it will be a habitation. If that place doesn't have everything you need, it will not be your habitation. The accommodations you viewed are not what you required or what you needed.

The Holy Spirit knows He has to have certain things to be comfortable. He will visit your home or visit your church and find out what is there. While He is visiting, you will feel His presence. You will feel His power. You will see some awesome things happen wherever He goes because He releases them in His presence. But then a week or so later, where is He? Where are the miracles? Where is the healing? Where is the prophecy? Where is the flow of God? Where is the glory of God?

What you desire as accommodations is not what the Holy Spirit desires as accommodations. What the Holy Spirit wants to have and to experience that makes Him comfortable is different than what makes you comfortable. You can't expect God to send His presence to take up habitation in your life, your home or your church and be comfortable with what you are comfortable with. "*Well, we like to sing these songs. We want to do things this way only. We want to do this. We want to do that.*" You may like to do all of that but what if they are not the accommodations the Holy Spirit likes? "*But I like to watch these movies and do these certain things. I like to watch violence.*"

Do we want His habitation or are we satisfied with a once a year visitation? With an occasional little chill down our spine? With an occasional whoop and holler? With an occasional little touch and little manifestation? Once in a while a little dream, a little vision?

I can't get enough of the presence of God, but I have found that I have to give Him what He likes and what He wants. Get close enough to Him and He will tell you what He doesn't like and it may not even be sin. "*Well, how much sin can I commit and still squeak into heaven? How far from God can I get and when I die still make it into glory*?" With that kind of life you don't have the manifestation of the habitation of God. You will miss out on the good things, on the greater things.

Let's do what it takes to accommodate Him. Then He will accompany us. He will show up and walk with us. He will show up and do all kinds of awesome things. All we have to do is walk in sync with Him. He will show you something and say, "*Do this.*" Start doing it and you will see manifestations.

In a meeting one time He spoke to me to loudly call out the word "*tragedy.*" I really didn't want to do it but He kept after me. At that time in my life I was a little fearful of man. Finally, I told the people that I was going to do something that might not make sense and began to scream out "*tragedy.*" After about three or four times a young girl came running to the altar. All day she had been saying that her life was a tragedy. She got saved that night.

It is time to walk in sync with the Holy Ghost, even if it means saying something that will make you look stupid in the natural. When I have done those kinds of things, the most awesome miracles have come out of it. Of course, I have a wrestling match with myself first.

I have determined that in anything the Lord requires of me, He is going to win. Sooner is much better than later. As many as are led by the

Spirit, they are the sons of God.[10] *"Led"* means to be in sync, in step with Him. It is *being* led, a constant process of constantly finding out what the Holy Ghost is doing, checking it out in the spirit and flowing wherever He is flowing. Walk in step with Him. If He takes two steps, you take two steps. If He stops, you stop. If He goes back one, you go back one. That is being led by the Spirit.

Jesus was led by the Spirit into the wilderness before He ever operated in the power of the Spirit in the wilderness. He was full of the Spirit before He was led by the Spirit. Then He returned in the power of the Spirit.[11]

You have to first be in step with the Spirit before you can be in the power of the Spirit. You have to constantly be led, constantly listening, looking. When you are, you are setting yourself up to operate in the power of the Spirit. Benny Hinn made this statement, "*The anointing doesn't come because you heard God. The anointing comes because you obeyed what you heard.*" There are people who hear but never obey and there is no anointing.

<u>You are not anointed because you hear God. You are anointed because you obey what you heard.</u> When you obey, you have moved out of the natural realm into the supernatural realm because you have stepped into being led by the Spirit, which then takes you into the power of the Spirit.

Jesus spoke only to the people what the Spirit of God said to speak. He laid hands only on the ones the Spirit said to and that is why He never had a failure. There have been times I have wanted to lay hands on people and the Holy Spirit would not lead me to do it. When I did anyway, I never saw anything happen. There was no fruit in it.

Jesus went to the Pool of Bethesda, which was the hospital of the day, and only one man was healed. Some people want to go into every hospital, lay hands on every sick person and empty the hospitals. No, you don't, unless the Holy Spirit leads you and you are in sync with Him. If

---

[10] Romans 8:14

[11] This story starts with Luke 4:1 and continues through the chapter.

you are not in sync with Him, you are not going to have His power. We think that because we have the gift of healing, we can lay hands on everybody and get them all healed. No, you can't. If the Holy Ghost is not leading you, there will be no fruit in it.

I don't witness to everybody. I am led by the Spirit. Jesus didn't even witness to everybody. But He did say, "*I need to go to Samaria. There is a woman at the well there that I have seen by the Spirit of God. The Spirit is leading me to be there at noon. I have an appointment with the Spirit of God. When I get in sync with Him, then the power of God will be available to me to minister supernaturally and see her life changed. Then a whole city will come to me.*"[12]

There have been times when I have been around someone that the Lord would tell me to say something and I would. Other times, I would hear, "*Don't say a thing. You will only be casting your pearls before swine.*"

Be led by the Spirit. The only way to do that is to be sensitive enough to find out where He is and what He is doing. We can keep ourselves from being worn out in the flesh by not doing dead works. It would be dead work if the Holy Spirit didn't lead us. The only way to have fruit is to be led by the Spirit.

---

[12] Luke 4:4-30

THE LAW OF PERCEPTION

There are six elements of perception. If you don't have them, you are not operating in the full perception that God wants you to operate in. Without perception you will not get anything because you won't know there is anything to get. If you don't know there is something available, you won't go after it. <u>Or, if you don't know the value of a thing, you won't treat it as a treasure.</u>

God wants us to come into a place where we can perceive the treasures of God, where we can perceive what is available, where we can perceive what is in front of us and know what is of value. If you don't know what is of value, you won't treat things of value as valuable. If you don't treat them as valuable you won't really possess those things. You will trample them under your feet, walk on as if they are nothing and get no benefit from it.

Failure to Receive

The first element of perception is: What you fail to perceive you fail to receive.

Matthew 13:13-15; ***"Therefore speak I to them in parables: because they seeing see not; and hearing they hear not, neither do they understand. And in them is fulfilled the prophecy of Esaias, which saith, By hearing ye shall hear, and shall not understand; and seeing ye shall see, and shall not perceive: For this people's heart is waxed gross, and their ears are dull of hearing, and their eyes they have closed; lest at any time they should see with their eyes, and hear with their ears, and should understand with their heart, and should be converted*** [changed]***, and I should heal them."***

Having eyes but not seeing, refers to spiritual perception. It is acting like a carnal, natural, mortal person who doesn't have a spirit man. You are operating everything by the natural. You don't know what is available, if there is anything beyond your own nose or beyond your own grasp in the natural realm. Therefore, you don't get it. You won't be changed and won't be healed.

If there is a lack in our lives, it is because there is a lack of perception. What you fail to perceive, you fail to receive. If you fail to receive something then there is lack in that area of your life.

We all need more spiritual perception, more spiritual insight. If there is a part of your life where you are not getting your full healing or your finances are not turned around yet, an area where the enemy has gotten in, an area where you are not seeing the full victory that you need, it is due to a lack of perception. Again, if you can perceive it, you can receive it. If you can catch the perception of it, your life will change, your situation will change and you will be healed of whatever you need healing of.

We need God to anoint our perception. Revelation 3:18 tells us of the need for our eyes to be anointed with eye salve so that we can see. Without the eye salve of God we are not going to perceive things. We are simply going to see things from a natural standpoint. We will never see things from the spiritual standpoint and therefore will never get the reception, never receive what we need from the Lord.

Level of Reception

The second element is that the level of perception is the level of reception. If you perceive something in a particular way that is how you will receive it. If you perceive to only a certain degree, that is the degree to which you will receive.

The story of the woman at the well is a story about perception. Jesus went to a woman who had a wrong perception, a lack of perception and He began to change it. She perceived Him as a Jew and wanted to know why He, a Jew, wanted to talk to her, a Samaritan. She also wanted to know why He would ask her for water. He began to increase her perception by telling her that He was not *just* a Jew and that He had water that she knew not of. He also told her that if she could perceive who He was, she would be asking Him for living water. In effect, Jesus was telling her that her perception would change what she received and the level at which she received.

Jesus went on to talk to her about some situations in her own personal life and she told Him that she perceived He was a prophet. As she picked up a little more perception and began to perceive Him as a prophet, she was able to receive Him as a prophet. Then, she could begin to ask Him some questions to get direction for her life about worship.

Jesus didn't stop there, but began to increase her perception even more. She went from first perceiving Him as a Jew, then as a prophet, and finally as the Messiah. When He got to the point where she believed that He truly was the Messiah, she totally received from Him. She ran into the town and told everyone that He was the Messiah.

John 4:29; ***"Come, see a man, which told me all things that ever I did: is not this the Christ?"***

The whole city came out.

I want you to see that all of this was based on levels of perception. If we only perceive ministries on certain levels then those are the only levels we will receive anything from them on. Some places only receive me as a prophet and that is the only way they will receive from me. They will not receive any teaching I do because they do not perceive me as a teacher, even though I flow in teaching. Other places perceive me as an evangelist. A lot of souls will get saved in those meetings and I will preach fiery messages like an evangelist.

Your level of perception is your level of reception.

Lost Perception

The third element is: What you don't perceive will leave.

Luke 19:41-44; ***"And when he was come near, he beheld the city, and wept over it, Saying, If thou hadst known, even thou, at least in this thy day, the things which belong unto thy peace! but now they are hid from thine eyes. For the days shall come upon thee, that thine enemies shall cast a trench about thee, and compass thee round, and keep thee in on every side, And shall lay thee even with the ground, and thy children within thee; and they shall not leave in thee one stone upon another;***

because thou <u>knewest not</u> [have no perception of] ***the time of thy visitation."***

"Knewest not" refers to perception. Because they could not perceive, they would not know the time of visitation. What you don't perceive will leave. When God sends ministry to you and you don't receive it, it will leave.

I was involved with a ministry in Texas for three years. Every service we saw cripples get up out of wheelchairs and walk. The blind would see. The deaf would hear. Cancers and tumors would fall off of people. It was amazing. But it got to the point where the people would begin to yawn. They were looking for something else to happen because there was a lack of perception. They couldn't perceive who God had sent and there came a day when that ministry was no longer there.

When God sends a ministry among you, even a pastor, you have to perceive that ministry or it will leave. You have a season during which God will test you to see if you will embrace a ministry. If you do, then there will not be a leaving but a cleaving, an embracing, a continuation. If you can't receive it, you won't cling to it.

Let me give you this illustration. Someone gave my wife a ring that had a pink stone on it. She thought it was a play ring so she gave it to her niece. Someone else looked at the ring and took it to a jewelry store. They found out that the ring was worth thirty-two hundred dollars. The stone was called pink ice. She couldn't perceive it because she didn't know the value of what she had. What you can't perceive will leave.

Jesus walked among the people in Jerusalem and they didn't perceive who He was because He didn't come in royal garments. He was not the high priest in the synagogue. They couldn't perceive Him because He didn't come in the package that they thought that kind of worth would come in. Almost all of us have that kind of attitude. We can't perceive what is in somebody because they are not in the package we thought they would be in.

I am sure they thought that of John the Baptist also. Here he comes screaming, out of the wilderness with honey dripping off his beard. They probably wondered who that wild man was and how could they receive anything from him.

We must perceive and cleave to that which is good.

1 Thessalonians 5:21; ***"Prove all things; hold fast that which is good."***

When you have proven it in the spirit realm and it is good, hang on to it. When it is around, cling to it, draw from it, bless it, be a part of it. It will only continue and increase.

Perception and Impartation

The fourth element is: What you can perceive in your leaders you can achieve in your life. Your leaders are the imparters. They are your spiritual mom and dad.

Philippians 4:9; ***"Those things, which ye have both learned, and received, and heard, and seen*** [perceived] ***in me, do: and the God of peace shall be with you."***

You can only do what you have perceived in your leaders. You can only do something because you have something. If someone has a healing ministry it is because of something they have. You have to have something to do something. Silver and gold have I none but such as I have give I thee.[13] Again, you can only do something because you have something.

You have to perceive what I have before you can do what I do. You have to perceive that there is a certain level of faith. You have to perceive that there is a certain revelation. You have to perceive that there is a certain positioning I have. You have to perceive that there is a certain connectivity that I have done. You have to perceive all the elements that have enabled me to do what I do. You can't do it until you have perceived it.

What you perceive in your leaders you can achieve in your life.

---

[13] Acts 3:6

Perception and Reception

Element five: If you perceive the five-fold ministry you will receive from them. If you can perceive who they are, you can receive from what they are. Remember, what I am, is what I do.

2 Kings 2:9; ***"And it came to pass, when they were gone over, that Elijah said unto Elisha, Ask what I shall do for thee, before I be taken away from thee. And Elisha said, I pray thee, let a double portion of thy spirit be upon me."***

Elisha had already perceived something.

2 Kings 2:10; ***"And he said, Thou hast asked a hard thing"***

Sometimes people don't know what to ask for. If you don't know what the question is, you never get the answer. I was with a prophetess one time that the Lord had connected us to and began to ask her how she heard from the Lord for people. She told me that sometimes she would be saying something while standing in front of someone and realize it was for that person. Other times there would be a light or illumination over a person and she would feel like that person really must have a word from God. I thought "*How cool.*" That cleared up a lot of things concerning the prophetic for me because I could ask the right questions. Sometimes we have to have enough perception to know what to ask.

2 Kings 2:10; ***"And he said, Thou hast asked a hard thing: nevertheless, if thou see me when I am taken from thee, it shall be so unto thee; but if not, it shall not be so."***

"If thou see me", you can have it. If you can't see me, you can't have it. Did Elisha see him?

2 Kings 2:11-12; ***"And it came to pass, as they still went on, and talked, that, behold, there appeared a chariot of fire, and horses of fire, and parted them both asunder; and Elijah went up by a whirlwind into heaven. And Elisha saw it, and he cried, My father, my father, the chariot of Israel, and the horsemen thereof. And he saw him no more: and he took hold of his own clothes, and rent them in two pieces."***

Elijah said, "*If you see me,*" and he saw it. Elijah did not say, "*If you see my mantles when I am taken up,*" but he said, "*If you see me.*" To see means to perceive. "*If you can perceive me when I am taken up.*" What did Elisha perceive? He perceived him as a father and cried out "*My father, my father.*"

"*Father*" in the Hebrew means my inheritor, the one who has something to give me. It is somebody I have submitted to, someone who has authority, a progenitor. A progenitor is someone who has something to give and who has a father's heart, a fathering anointing.

Elijah was telling Elisha that if he could perceive him when he went, then Elisha could have what he wanted. But if he couldn't perceive Elijah, he couldn't have it. How true that is in the spirit.

In other words, you have to perceive the five-fold ministry that God has placed over your life and perceive who they are to you, or you can't get anything from them. Elisha perceived who Elijah was to him as someone who had something to give, someone who was over him, a progenitor, and he got the double portion.

So few people ever grasp this. They don't know who their spiritual heads are. They don't know who their progenitors are. They don't know who their inheritors are. They have no one and are very limited in what they have. You can have your own anointing but that is a measure. When you connect with others you don't just have what you have, but what they have also. That is the double portion.

You get a part of what every minister you connect with has. Your life is increased way beyond your little bit of oil. You can be proud of your little bit of oil and stay with it the rest of your days if you want to. I am not happy with just a little measure. I want the whole barrel. I want everything God has. I want to connect with other people and get the anointing that is upon them. I want to come into levels greater than I have ever known, greater than I have ever seen.

We are so careful and that is okay. But, we are looking for absolute perfection in flesh and we will never find it. You can find my feet of clay and my faults, but it doesn't mean that I don't have an anointing and a mantle to give. Every minister I have ever served had feet of clay, was housed in flesh and made mistakes. However, they each had something I needed and I had to come to the place where I didn't look at the flesh. I had to say, "*My father, my father*."

"*That means your heavenly father*," you might say. Don't you understand that there is a body of Christ and that it has fathers? There is a heavenly father and there are spiritual fathers in the Lord. Paul said that there were not many fathers and yet, he called himself one.[14] The apostles and prophets have always been called fathers.

When scripture says not to call anyone father, it is referring to calling anyone on earth your heavenly father.[15] See how misinformed we have been? I am not anyone's heavenly father, but I have something to give. I have some mantles and some things to impart, but if you can't perceive it, you can't get it.

The devil has the job of keeping you from ever connecting. You may think that you and Jesus have your own thing going, but that is a lie from the devil. It is the body and Jesus. Yes, you can have a personal experience however you are a part of something much bigger than you. When Jesus comes back, it won't be for just one person, but for His whole church.

What Perception and Reception Look Like

The last element I want to show you from the scriptures is what perception and reception look like.

2 Kings 4:8-9; *"And it fell on a day, that Elisha passed to Shunem, where was a great woman; and she constrained him to eat bread. And so it was, that as oft as he passed by, he turned in thither to eat bread. And she said unto her husband, Behold now, I perceive that this is an holy man of God, which passeth by us continually."*

---

[14] 1 Corinthians 4:15
[15] Matthew 23:9

Her perception is that he is a holy man of God. What does she do with it? What are you doing with your perception?

2 Kings 4:10; *"Let us make a little chamber, I pray thee, on the wall; and let us set for him there a bed, and a table, and a stool, and a candlestick: and it shall be, when he cometh to us, that he shall turn in thither."*

Here is her response. If this is a holy man of God, she is going to have to make room for him. Are you making room on your calendar for the man of God when he comes to visit? Are you providing for, blessing the man of God when he does come?

If she had not provided for the prophet, God would have had someone else in another location take care of him.

2 Kings 4:11-14; *"And it fell on a day, that he came thither, and he turned into the chamber, and lay there. And he said to Gehazi his servant, Call this Shunammite. And when he had called her, she stood before him. And he said unto him, Say now unto her, Behold, thou hast been careful for us with all this care; what is to be done for thee? wouldest thou be spoken for to the king, or to the captain of the host? And she answered, I dwell among mine own people. And he said, What then is to be done for her?"*

When you start perceiving and receiving the ministry God will start speaking to that man of God to find a need you have and to meet it.

We come to get our need met when we should come to meet a need. We should come to perceive and connect because it is through the perceiving and connecting that our needs will be met.

So, this sixth element asks, "*What do perception and reception look like?*" They look like a person who perceives and then responds to that perception by responding to the person they perceive has the anointing. You respond to that person by loving them, by connecting with them, by blessing them in whatever way you can. God knows what you can and cannot do. He will always have you respond in some way. That is how it works.

What you don't know the value of, you won't treat as a treasure.

COVENANT CONNECTIONS

Covenant connections are very much a part of impartations. Nothing can be imparted without a covenant connection because that is what enables impartation to take place. We will look at how covenant connections work as well as how they start and progress.

I don't believe we understand how to connect here in America. We know how to sit in a service, how to listen to a tape, as well as how to draw something out. While more than fifty percent of marriages end up in divorce, it is a larger percentage in the church because we don't understand covenant connections.

Proximity

Covenant connections are relationships. It is not just receiving from a ministry but building a relationship with that ministry.

Romans 1:11; ***"For I long to see you, that I may impart unto you some spiritual gift, to the end ye may be established;"***

Notice, Paul said he longed to see them. The *seeing you* has to do with being with somebody, proximity. It is being close enough to look in their eyes, close enough to see their face and their facial features, their expressions. Maybe you will shake their hand or hug their neck. The release of love and the interaction of one with another is important.

Romans 1:12; ***"That is, that I may be comforted together with you by the mutual faith both of you and me."***

Covenant connection has to do with proximity. You cannot have a close covenant relationship if you never see that person. In the high tech world we live in today with computers, radio and television we can hear good ministry, can watch them on television, and can see them on the Internet. That may be a form of a covenant, but it is not what Paul was talking about. There is something missing.

I have been in services, in situations with other ministers where they didn't really know me and I didn't know them. I just hung out a little bit. That is not a close intimate covenant relationship. I think it is a powerful thing when God gives you the opportunity to connect with a ministry on a little more of an intimate level to where they know your face, know your name, have interacted with you and you with them. You love them and they love you. What an opportunity that is.

God wants us to build a connection, a covenant relationship with people. It can't just be a minister trying to do that. It has to be people who want it to happen as well. All Elijah did was come, throw his mantle around the shoulder of Elisha and leave town. Elisha had to go after him.

One pastor I know told his people that he knew many of them were getting upset because he didn't shake their hand, didn't know their name or even who they were. He had a church of several hundred of people. He told them they had to make themselves known, to press into him. They should not to leave immediately after church, but should shake his hand and tell him who they were. They should not expect him to do everything. He looked at several hundred people and asked how was he to do it all. If they wanted the relationship, they had to be the ones to press in.

When looking at covenant relationships, let's look at the crowds of people. Jesus ministered to the multitudes, but it wasn't a very close intimate relationship. Then there were the seventy who were a little bit closer to Jesus. They knew a little bit more about Him, spent a little more time with Him than the multitudes did. Next were the twelve. They hung out with Him everywhere He went, stayed with and traveled with Him. Next, there were the three who were always pressing into Him. They hung out with Him more. When He went up on the mountain to pray, they were there. Last, there was one who was hugging on Him twenty-four/seven. John called himself the disciple the Lord loved. In reality he was the disciple who loved the Lord.

The Lord loves everybody the same. The relationship depends on the person. You have to press in. John pressed in to always be close to Jesus. A covenant relationship has to be one that you pursue.

You, first of all, have to know that God wants a connection. Then you have to know what kind of connection is there and you have to press in for the connection. *You* have to press in. *You* have to decide what you are going to do.

You can get some things from the Internet or from television. But there are some things you cannot get without a face-to-face with ministries. Somehow we have to get close enough to rub shoulders with them a little bit. Every time they are around, we should be where they are as much as possible. By doing that there is a release of something in the spirit. I feel it many times. When I am ministering, I will look into people's faces and feel something shoot out of my spirit into theirs. You don't get that kind of thing watching television or listening to a tape. Paul didn't say, "*I am going to send you some writings and they will give an impartation.*" He longed to see them that he might impart.

I am not saying you can't get something from books, television programs, cassettes or CDs. You can. But you can't get the full load, the high level of intimate things being released except by proximity. How close are those ministries to you? Are you pressing in?

Trustworthiness

The next element about covenant connections is what I call trustworthiness. In order to release impartations there has to be trustworthiness on the part of those who desire to receive from the ministry.

2 Timothy 2:1-2; *"Thou therefore, my son, be strong in the grace that is in Christ Jesus. And the things that thou hast heard of me among many witnesses, the same commit thou to faithful men, who shall be able to teach others also."*

"Commit" literally means to deposit or to impart. Timothy was to deposit or impart to faithful men. Faithful means trustworthy. Faithful men have a track record. They have been around long enough to show they are trustworthy. There is faithfulness, a connection there. Paul told Timothy to impart to faithful men, trustworthy men who had been close to him, had been right there for him, had pressed into him.

Jesus didn't impart everything to everybody. He gave to His twelve disciples because they were there with Him all the time. He gave more to the three than He did the twelve. He gave more to the one than He did the three. It all had to do with faithfulness and pressing in, staying close.

You have to understand and perceive before you can receive, before you press in.

Supply

We have to be knit together by supply. What will knit you to me and me to you is the fact that I am going to impart something to you. I am going to release a supply of something in the spirit to you. At the same time you are going to release a supply of something to me – prayer, strength, finances. That supply going back and forth is what is going to knit us together.

Ephesians 4:16; *"From whom the whole body fitly joined together and compacted by that which every joint supplieth, according to the effectual working in the measure of every part, maketh increase of the body unto the edifying of itself in love."*

Joined together by supply. Let's look at that verse in the Amplified.

Ephesians 4:16; *"For because of Him the whole body (the church, in all its various parts closely) joined and firmly knit together by the joints and ligaments with which it is supplied, when each part [with power adapted to its need] is working properly (in all its functions), grows to full maturity, building itself up in love."* (Amplified Bible)

Each joint is being knit together by supply. What knits us together is what I release to you in the spirit and what you release to me. Isn't that awesome?

That supply is the supernatural things the ministry is releasing to you and the supernatural that you are releasing through your prayer, your love, and through your finances back to the ministry. There can't be a connection if only one joint is releasing something and the other joint is not. The connection only comes when it works both ways.

The ministry imparts something to your life and you are thrilled. You, then, turn around and pray for, love, support that ministry with finances and prayer. The flow between the joints is working.

There can't be a covenant connection if it is only one sided. It can't be you doing everything and the ministry giving you nothing. Let's say you are sending to the ministry but you never receive anything spiritually from them. That is not a covenant connection. It is also not a covenant connection if you are receiving spiritual things, but are not contributing, releasing, praying, supporting. There has to be a supernatural release back and forth.

The Tale of Two Sisters

Naomi and her family had left Bethlehem of Judea because there was no bread in the town. Going to a far country to live, the sons married women of the area. While they were there the men got sick and died. Naomi heard bread was back in Bethlehem and decided to return there. Now, there came a time to make a decision as to what the daughter-in-laws would do. They needed to get on with their lives and remarry since they were still young.

Ruth 1:14-15; *"And they lifted up their voice, and wept again: and Orpah kissed her mother in law; but Ruth clave unto her. And she said, Behold, thy sister in law is gone back unto her people, and unto her gods: return thou after thy sister in law."*

Orpah kissed her mother-in-law and went on her way. Ruth hung on to her mother-in-law, connected to her. There was a covenant between them.

Ruth 1:16-17; *"And Ruth said, Intreat me not to leave thee, or to return from following after thee: for whither thou goest, I will go; and where thou lodgest, I will lodge: thy people shall be my people, and thy God my God: Where thou diest, will I die, and there will I be buried: the LORD do so to me, and more also, if ought but death part thee and me."*

We don't hear of that kind of covenant connection, that connection of the heart here in America. We have such an independent spirit that we can't even connect in marriage that way. We can't connect in churches that way either. We wonder why we don't get the full measure of impartations, why we don't get inheritances and mantles. There have to be some connections.

Ruth 1:22; *"So Naomi returned, and Ruth the Moabitess, her daughter in law, with her, which returned out of the country of Moab: and they came to Bethlehem in the beginning of barley harvest."*

Because Ruth returned with Naomi in covenant, it brought her to the harvest. Covenant connections will bring you to a harvest.

Ruth 2:1; *"And Naomi had a kinsman of her husband's, a mighty man of wealth, of the family of Elimelech; and his name was Boaz."*

When you connect in covenant connections, they will bring you into the land of harvest and connect you with the Boazs. Anointed ministry will bring you to the harvest if you are in covenant with them, will cleave to them instead of kissing them and walking away. Many want to tell the man of God how much they love them, kiss him on the cheek, but not come around again for years. They got what they perceived they needed or wanted from the ministry and are gone.

Then there are people who have the attitude of Ruth. They will cleave to, hug and hang on to the ministry. They consider the ministry to be part of their life. The ministry will not get away from them no matter where it goes. They will stay connected to, love, support, and pray for that ministry and that ministry will bring them to the harvest. The ministry will also connect them to the Boazs they need.

God has some people, some situations where there is wealth. He has some people who know how to bless you beyond anything you have ever imagined or thought. They are looking at you because you are being positioned, due to your covenant connection, with the anointed apostles and prophets of God. They see that you are faithful, that you are covenant, that there is anointing flowing out of you.

Some don't understand that there is a difference between anointing flowing into your little cup and a source of something that has a continual flow through you. When you connect with ministries on a continual basis you have a continual flow, a life-giving flow. Whoever you are connected with is who is flowing through you right now. The Boazs see that.

One sister kissed the ministry and took off. The other one clung and said, "*I am not leaving you. I am hanging on to you. You are a part of my life.*"

Ruth kept going to the fields, gleaning and bringing back what she could to Naomi. She was always bringing offerings to Naomi, always blessing her and wasn't in lack because of it. She wasn't torn down, but was lifted up and blessed. Ruth ended up becoming very wealthy and that is not the entire story. She married Boaz and had a child who was the great grandpa to David, the king of Israel.

Your connection will cause you to give birth to kingly anointing. It will cause you to bring kingly power into the earth through you. Out of your loins will come kingly power. Your children, grandchildren and great grandchildren will walk in power and glory in the earth. It depends on who you are connecting to, cleaving to.

Are You Standing in the Door?

We are going to look at a lady who created a door for the prophet and it became her doorway to her destiny.

2 Kings 4:8-11; ***"And it fell on a day, that Elisha passed to Shunem, where was a great*** [wealthy] ***woman; and she constrained him to eat bread. And so it was, that as oft as he passed by, he turned in thither to eat bread. And she said unto her husband, Behold now, I perceive that this is an holy man of God, which passeth by us continually. Let us make a little chamber, I pray thee, on the wall; and let us set for him there a bed, and a table, and a stool, and a candlestick: and it shall be, when he cometh to us, that he shall turn in thither. And it fell on a day, that he came thither, and he turned into the chamber, and lay there."***

If you are going to make a chamber, there will be a doorway into it.

In Israel they have flat roofed houses so they build houses on top of houses as a way of doing their additions. There will be a staircase going up the side to the next level. A doorway will also be there for the house on that level.

The woman made a doorway so that the man of God could enter the little house that she made for him.

2 Kings 4:12-15; ***"And he said to Gehazi his servant, Call this Shunammite. And when he had called her, she stood before him. And he said unto him, Say now unto her, Behold, thou hast been careful for us with all this care; what is to be done for thee? wouldest thou be spoken for to the king, or to the captain of the host? And she answered, I dwell among mine own people. And he said, What then is to be done for her? And Gehazi answered, Verily she hath no child, and her husband is old. And he said, Call her. And when he had called her, she stood in the door."***

What door? The door she made for the man of God. The entrance she made for the prophet became her entrance into her destiny. What you make happen for others, God makes happen for you. If you honor others, God will honor you. That is a scriptural key.

She came into covenant relationship saying she was going to bless the man of God so that all of his needs would always be met. Making sure there was a place for the prophet in her life, she set aside time and finances for the prophet to make sure he had a resting place.

She was going to do all she could to create a situation that would allow the prophetic to have entryway into her life. The doorway she made for the prophet was the doorway she would walk through for her destiny. Remember, what you make happen for others, God makes happen for you.

She stood in the door and the prophet asked what she needed. Did she want a position in government? He could give it to her through the prophetic. Some do not understand the power of the prophetic. It is creative.

Did the woman need something taken care of legally? He could go to the captain of the host. He could get the police on it.

She answered that she dwelt among her own people and did not need all of that. Again the prophet asked what she needed. Gehazi answered that she had never had a child. While she was standing in the door she created for the prophet, he said she would have a child according to the time of life. Covenant connection comes because of the door you create.

You have to create a place in your heart for the prophet. The house, table and chair represent that place. You say you need the prophetic in your life? Open up a part of your heart for the prophetic. The door you open is the door you will enter through to the things God has destined you to do.

Covenant connections will change your life, but you have to understand and operate those connections. What you make happen for the men and women of God, God will make happen for you. He will open the greatest blessing for your life. God enables the prophets to see your destiny when you connect with them, but only *if* you can connect with them. Through that connection they have the power to create with their words. Not only are they able to perceive what your future is but they can create it with their words.

The prophet's reward is only for covenant people. It doesn't come to people who are not in covenant. The prophet's reward is for those who are in covenant, have opened their heart and make a connection. Then whatever the prophet prophesies will come to pass. That is the prophet's reward.

The reward is the prophet being able to look into your destiny, see it and then create it with words. They can bring something to pass early that could take another ten, fifteen or twenty years to happen. Through your connection, they can kick it in to another gear and bring it into another dimension of time. What would take you forty years to do can be done in ten to fifteen just by connecting to the prophets. That is called prophetic acceleration.

We have to perceive. If you can perceive it, you can receive it. Remember, you lose what you don't perceive. It goes past you and you never get it. It is gone forever.

HOW TO RECEIVE IMPARTATIONS

The Holy Spirit is looking for people He can trust so that He can release the seed of His Word into their hearts. He is looking for people who will birth His plans and purposes in prayer, through intercession, through obedience, through praise and through following the voice of the Spirit. When you birth the Word, it will become flesh.

I want to share with you the principles of coming into impartations and what you have to do to position yourself for them. What people have determines whether they are successful or not. The mantles they possess, the glory that they operate in and under will determine success or failure. Be careful who you hook up with and make sure you look for character not just for power. Look for someone who has Christ-like attitudes and Christ-like virtues. Look for someone who thinks like Jesus would think and lives like Jesus would live if He were walking on this earth. Look for someone who lives a dedicated, consecrated, sold out life and walks in holiness. They do not just talk about it. It is not that they don't ever make a mistake in life, they just don't want to. They are not out trying to sin or living a lifestyle of sinning.

When you are looking to receive an impartation from a ministry, you should be hooking up with a ministry that has something you need. Each of the five-fold has an anointing, an ability given to them by God. I call it equipment. In a vision I had one time, I saw the five-fold with what looked like shopping bags. They would carry them into the house of God and preach. Then they would carry them back out. Again, they would carry them in and carry them back out. They were getting tired of carrying this stuff around all the time. The Lord said that what was wrong was they didn't know they had something for the people. The five-fold ministry has to realize that what they have is not for them. No, everything in their shopping bag is for the people. Everything I possess is for me to give to you. Every gifting, every anointing, every blessing, every good thing that is in me belongs to the body of Christ. I am supposed to give the equipment, to impart it to you. But, I can't impart anything to you unless you position yourself to receive it.

There are five ways for you to position yourself to receive the impartation. Prayer is part of it, but it is more than prayer. Everything that you need in God is in the five-fold ministry. God will connect you with the five-fold ministry if you will pray. Your heart will connect with them because you know that you love them. You don't know how you love them but you do. The five-fold will have the same love for you. There is a mutual connection. It is like the heart of Jonathan being knit to the heart of David. They loved each other dearly. At the same time there was impartation that was released to one another. We have to begin to see that God is going to build relationships in the body of Christ. He is going to build relationships with the five-fold ministry.

I remember the first time I met Jeff Johns. I loved him like he was my father. He loved me like I was his son, even though we are both the same age. The Lord spoke to me and told me that spiritual fatherhood and sonship is different than natural fatherhood and sonship. It is not based on natural age. It is not even based on giftings or anointings. It is based on authority. I felt in the spirit that this man had a level of authority beyond where I was. He told me one time that there was a knitting of our hearts together and asked if I felt the same thing. Yes, I did. He went on to tell me that there is no contract in the natural. He was not asking me to sign some papers and he wasn't going to sign any papers. It was a heart matter and was stronger than anything on paper. That is awesome.

It was the same way when I met Apostle Fred Pine. There was a connection between these men and myself. If you will pray, God will give you that same kind of connection with all of the five-fold ministry. You don't just need an apostle only, though you need an apostle. You don't just need a prophet only in your life, but you need a prophet. You don't just need a pastor, but you need a pastor. It is the same thing with the evangelist and the teacher. You need to connect to all the five-fold ministry. Each one has something that the others cannot give you. If you will pray and be open to connect, ask God to make the right connections, He will because that is His will.

Be a Disciple

Luke 11:1; ***"And it came to pass, that, as he was praying in a certain place, when he ceased, one of his disciples said unto him, Lord, teach us to pray, as John also taught his disciples."***

Notice, the disciple did not ask the Lord to teach them how to pray, but to teach them to pray. To teach someone to pray means to bring them into the ability to pray. There is something awesome about prayer. If you can get into the flow and get an impartation of a prayer mantle, you will go into prayer over and over. It will motivate you, draw you, and empower you. It will give you an unction to function. When you get the unction to function, then you can go to the Word and get teaching on how to pray. You will learn what scriptures to use, how to use your faith in prayer, how to move into praying in tongues.

Most Christians can tell you how to pray. They will tell you that you should ask in faith. They can tell you about petitioning prayer. They can tell you about different kinds of prayer that they may not actually be praying themselves. Most of the church today knows the how-to of prayer, but they are not brought into the actual praying mode. They don't have a prayer mantle. When you have a prayer mantle you are a doer. You are not just someone who knows about it, but someone who does it. There is a difference. You can know about something or you can be doing something. The doer is the one who is blessed. It is not just someone who knows something. The bible says that we are self-deceived when we know something, but don't do it. We have moved into deception.[16]

The church as a whole has been deceived. They think that because they know about prayer, they must have the anointing of it. You don't have the anointing because you have the revelation on something, unless that revelation brings you to motivation. The motivation brings you to actualization. Actualization brings you into manifestation. Then you are blessed. James 1:2 says that you are blessed in your deed if you do the Word.

---

[16] James 1:23-24

The disciples came to Jesus because they heard Him pray. It starts with coming into discipleship. Before you can get impartations, you have to become a disciple. A disciple is a disciplined learner, a disciplined follower. In other words, you must hook up with a ministry long enough. It can't be a hit-and-miss thing. It can't be, "*Well, I heard so and so five years ago and haven't heard him since.*" You have not really hooked up with that ministry. To hook up and be a disciple of a ministry means you are in regular prayer for that ministry. You are listening to their tapes, reading their books. You are sitting under that ministry as often as you are able to. You are positioning yourself. Those disciples who heard Jesus pray came and asked Him to teach them. They tried and couldn't seem to get into it.

Think about it. They had been with Jesus and heard Him pray, but they had not yet received the impartation. It takes time to hook up with a ministry and get everything they have. Elisha hooked up with Elijah for twenty years before he ever prophesied to anybody, before he moved in any power, before he did any miracles. After twenty years, he finally got the mantle and did twice the miracles. Elijah did eleven. Elisha did twenty-two, exactly twice the miracles. But, it took twenty years to get it all. We can't even hook up with a ministry for five days. How can we expect to get any impartation? You can't get it on a short-term basis. You have to hook up until it manifests. You have to hook up until it is released.

It starts with the word disciple. Disciple means disciplined learner, disciplined follower. The word discipline is there. Disciple is a hard word because you have to be self-disciplined to be a disciple. Jesus came to those men and asked them to be His disciple. To do that, they had to follow. They had to discipline themselves every day to follow Jesus. There is no doubt they had many temptations. Maybe they had ministered all day, prayed all night with the Lord and the next day they were tired. I am sure some of them may have asked if they could stay on and rest. They would catch up with Him the next week. Maybe they felt they needed a little vacation, would like to do some extra fishing. Maybe they wanted to get out on the beach and get some sun.

In order to get impartation, it is going to cost you something. At this point, we are not just talking finances. It is going to cost you time. It is going to be inconvenient for you to be at the meeting. It is going to be inconvenient for you to sit under that ministry. It is going to be inconvenient for you to hear the Word all the time under that ministry and receive everything they have. But, inconvenience in the end will pay off and it is called discipleship.

Let me show you the power of this because it is so awesome. Jesus said that the disciple can have everything that the master, the teacher has.

Matthew 10:24-25a; *"The disciple is not above his master, nor the servant above his lord. It is enough for the disciple that he be as his master, and the servant as his lord."*

"Master" means an instructor who has mastered something in the spirit. It is like having a Master's Degree in the spirit. Maybe they have mastered faith. Maybe they have mastered prayer. Maybe they have mastered in the gifts of the spirit. Maybe they have mastered in bible study or mastered something else in the spirit.

The disciple who has hooked up with the one who has mastered something in the spirit can get everything that person has.

So, one of the ways of positioning yourself for an impartation is to become a disciple, a disciplined follower of those who have mastered certain things in the spirit. God has already knit your heart to them, so you love them and they love you. Because you are disciplined to listen, to follow, to pray and to be a part of that ministry then in time you will be just like them. You will be as the master, as one who has mastered it. You operate in the identically same anointing and power.

Let's look at what a disciple can get, what a disciple can have.

Matthew 10:5-8; *"These twelve Jesus sent forth, and commanded them, saying, Go not into the way of the Gentiles, and into any city of the Samaritans enter ye not: But go rather to the lost sheep of the house of Israel. And as ye go, preach, saying, The kingdom of heaven is at hand. Heal the sick, cleanse the lepers, raise the dead, cast out devils: freely ye have received, freely give."*

What did they freely receive? They were freely receiving mantles and divine abilities from the master.

Jesus is the master of all masters. Remember, a master is someone who has mastered a certain area in the spirit. It is like going through all twelve years of grade school, four years of high school, four years of college, get your bachelor's degree and then on to your masters. The next step would be your doctorate. In Jesus' time if they had their master's degree, they were called doctor. We are not talking about a natural degree, though, but a spiritual degree. You know if someone has a spiritual degree because they have the goods. They are flowing in it. You can see it. It is something they possess. It is something in their life.

It is important that you connect with people. Too many are trying to follow from far off. If you do, then you don't get a lot. The woman with the issue of blood pressed in and got everything she needed.

One pastor I know told his people, "*Don't expect me to press into you. You have to press into me.*" He had so many people who wanted him to disciple them that he had to tell them to press into him. He always stayed until everyone was gone and yet there were people who would get upset with him because he didn't shake their hand. They wanted him to come to them. He told his people they were as close to the five-fold ministry as they wanted to be. The decision was theirs and it had to be a heart thing. Jesus said, "*follow me*" and then He left. They had to follow Him. If they chose not to follow, He let them go.

Disciples not only connect with someone who has mastered something in the five-fold ministry, but then they go after it. They connect, first of all, with the heart. Then they will draw everything they can from that ministry. They will be in every service they can. They will be there to soak, be there to receive not just a word, but an impartation. The more often you can connect, the more you will get.

Do you know why John the Beloved called himself the disciple whom the Lord loved? It was because he loved the Lord more than the rest of them. He got so close to Jesus, got such an impartation that they couldn't kill him. By the way, that impartation was available to all the disciples. John died of natural causes, of old age. He was close to ninety years of age when he died, the only disciple that the devil couldn't kill. It was John's decision to draw near.

Be a Helper

Numbers 11:24-25; ***"And Moses went out, and told the people the words of the LORD, and gathered the seventy men of the elders of the people, and set them round about the tabernacle. And the LORD came down in a cloud, and spake unto him, and took of the spirit that was upon him, and gave it unto the seventy elders: and it came to pass, that, when the spirit rested upon them, they prophesied, and did not cease."***

These seventy men were the ones who helped Moses with the people, helped him judge them. They took the pressure off of Moses so that he didn't wear himself out doing all the ministry. They lifted the load, carried part of the weight.

The Lord took the spirit that rested upon Moses and gave it to the seventy elders. Are you catching this? That means the same anointing, the same abilities, the same prophetic power that was upon Moses.

Moses had some powerful prophetic ability. He would go in, hold out his rod and heaven and earth would respond to him. Remember the plagues? Remember when he held out his rod and the waters parted? Just think about all the signs, wonders and miracles. He had a strong Spirit of God upon him.

The elders who had helped lift the load, who worked with him in the ministry were the ones to whom the Lord gave the same prophetic power of signs, wonders and miracles. When He did that, they prophesied. They had never prophesied before. It did not cease, meaning it never stopped. They got what Moses had. As far as I am concerned, Moses had one of the strongest anointings in the bible for signs, wonders and miracles. He didn't just affect individuals but nations. That kind of anointing was given to seventy people who were willing to work with him in the ministry.

God is still doing it today for those who will connect with the ministries that God has connected them to. He will impart the same mantles, the same abilities, and the same anointings to those who are willing to lift the load.

Be a Spiritual Son

2 Kings 2:2; ***"And Elijah said unto Elisha, Tarry here, I pray thee; for the LORD hath sent me to Bethel. And Elisha said unto him, As the LORD liveth, and as thy soul liveth, I will not leave thee. So they went down to Bethel."***

It is important that when God shows you who you are to be connected to, you are not supposed to leave them. You are not supposed to disconnect until God tells you to. Even then, you had better make sure it is God and not just your emotions.

Elijah was a tough person to hang out with. He had an anger problem. He would get angry, call down fire and people would die.

That would be a tough person to follow. You would be wondering if the coffee was too hot or too cold. One wrong move and you might be a cinder on the ground.

God has connected me with some people in the ministry who were tough. They were hard on me, but because they were, I have a faith level now that I would have never had. During those times, I learned to believe God and to believe His Word. I achieved a faith level that has carried me through in the ministry. I learned principles that are still very effective in my life today.

We have to understand that if we are looking for a perfect five-fold minister to hook up with, we will never hook up. The thing you have to do is hear God. Who is God saying to hook up with? Be thankful if they are nice. Be thankful if there is a sweetness about them. Be thankful if they are not too tough, though sometimes the toughness is what you need.

2 Kings 2:4; ***"And Elijah said unto him, Elisha, tarry here, I pray thee; for the LORD hath sent me to Jericho. And he said, As the LORD liveth, and as thy soul liveth, I will not leave thee. So they came to Jericho."***

2 Kings 2:6; ***"And Elijah said unto him, Tarry, I pray thee, here; for the LORD hath sent me to Jordan. And he said, As the LORD liveth, and as thy soul liveth, I will not leave thee. And they two went on."***

2 Kings 2:9-10; ***"And it came to pass, when they were gone over, that Elijah said unto Elisha, Ask what I shall do for thee, before I be taken away from thee. And Elisha said, I pray thee, let a double portion of thy spirit be upon me. And he said, Thou hast asked a hard thing: nevertheless, if thou see me when I am taken from thee, it shall be so unto thee; but if not, it shall not be so."***

"If thou see me" is talking about perception. You can't receive anything that you can't perceive.

Are you perceiving the failure? Are you perceiving the flesh? Are you perceiving weakness? Do you have the gift of suspicion? The gift of suspicion is not the gift of discerning of spirits. It is being suspicious of every minister.

With discerning of spirits, everything may look right, but you feel something isn't. Or something may look wrong, but in the spirit it is right. You can't go by the natural. You have to go by the spirit.

2 Kings 2:11-12; ***"And it came to pass, as they still went on, and talked, that, behold, there appeared a chariot of fire, and horses of fire, and parted them both asunder; and Elijah went up by a whirlwind into heaven. And Elisha saw it, and he cried, My father, my father, the chariot of Israel, and the horsemen thereof. And he saw him no more: and he took hold of his own clothes, and rent them in two pieces."***

What was it that Elisha discerned? A father anointing. Elijah told him that if he could see him, discern him for who he really was to Elisha, then he could have the double portion. This is powerful if you can look at a spiritual ministry and say, *"There is a spiritual father in that person."*

That father anointing may be in someone who is younger than you. Some of the people who I see moving into things now are younger than I am. They are moving to a greater degree in things than I am. I can look at them and see a father anointing. I can look at them and see someone who can impart something to me.

I can recognize and perceive father anointings. And if I can perceive it, then I can receive it. It cannot be done fleshly, with natural eyes. If you go by the natural you will miss out.

"If thou see me when I am taken from thee..." *"See"* means to perceive. Elijah was saying, "*If you can perceive who I really am in the spirit then you can have the double portion of what I have. You can have what I have if you can perceive what I have, who I am in the spirit to you.*"

Signs, wonders and miracles were happening, but Elisha wasn't looking at that. He was looking at the man of God. There were chariots of fire, but he wasn't concerned about that. He said, "*My father, my father.*" The Hebrew word for father is *ab* and the Greek word is *pater*. It means the one who has something to give me. The one who has something I don't have. The one who has an inheritance. The one who is mature, a master in certain things in the spirit, who has something to impart to me.

You have to perceive when a man or woman of God, no matter what age they are, has something to impart to you or has mastered something in the spirit. If you can perceive, you can receive. It is time we look in the spirit realm.

"*My father, my father*" means I am a son. We need to understand what sonship means. You can't receive the inheritance until you become a son. There are a lot of spiritual fathers but are you a son to any of them? A son is one who won't leave a father.

In the story of the prodigal son, remember the son who didn't leave? When the prodigal left, he only got a portion of what the father had. The one who stayed as a faithful son and didn't leave the father, kept helping, kept working, kept connected got jealous when the other son finally came back. The father told him, "*Son, all that I have belongs to you. Everything I have is yours. At any moment you could throw yourself a party.*" He didn't tell him the prodigal son had only gotten a portion, but said that all that he had was his.

Sons get everything that the fathers have. That means you are faithful. Your heart is connected. There is a respect level. What you honor you draw near. What you dishonor you push away. You have to do whatever it takes to help you focus on giving honor where honor is due. God is the only one who deserves worship but there are ministers who deserve honor because of the price they paid, because of the position God has placed them in. If you honor that, you will be honoring God. Whatever you honor you attract to yourself. Whatever you dishonor you push away. So, a son who wants to get everything a father has must not dishonor the father. He must always respect the father while knowing that the father has frailties, has problems.

Be a Partner

The book of Philippians was written to a church that Paul had raised up. They became disciples, helpers, and sons. Then they became one other thing - partners.

Philippians 1:3-5; ***"I thank my God upon every remembrance of you, Always in every prayer of mine for you all making request with joy, For your fellowship in the gospel from the first day until now;"***

Fellowship in the Greek is *koinonia (koy-nohn-ee'-ah)* and it means partnership. Paul is saying that they hooked up as a partner from the very beginning. A partner is someone who has a part and takes part.

Philippians 1:6; ***"Being confident of this very thing, that he which hath begun a good work in you will perform it until the day of Jesus Christ:"***

Paul was confident that they were going to grow and mature in what God had started in them through his ministry. It would come to fruition, maturity. God would complete something in them.
Philippians 1:7; ***"Even as it is meet for me to think this of you all, because I have you in my heart; inasmuch as both in my bonds, and in***

the defence and confirmation of the gospel, ye all are partakers of my grace."

"Grace" in this verse means divine abilities, gifts and anointings. They were now a partaker of what he had. They were partaking of the same gifts, mantles and anointings. Paul told them they had his grace, his anointing, his divine ability.

Be a Partaker

Partners become partakers.

Remember the time when Jesus told the disciples to go fishing. They were to cast their net on the other side. When they did they got such a huge catch of fish that the boat began to sink. They had to call the other ships to come and help. The disciples wanted them to become partners and help bring in the load of fish.[17]

Fish can also represent souls being saved. A ministry throws out the net to win the lost, but there are so many people to win I can't get them all in my boat. I can't draw them all in by myself. I need partners. I need people who will pray for me and support me financially. I need people who care about what we are doing in the work of God and who want to be a part of reaching the lost. Those who are partners will be partakers of the same grace that I operate in.

Let's review. To receive an impartation you must become a disciple, be a helper of a ministry, become a spiritual son with ministry, and become a partner. Then God causes you to become a partaker.

God showed me these steps a few years ago. When I started doing it, I picked up different mantles. I remember picking up the mantles of the word of knowledge. I picked up mantles of creative miracles – tumors disappearing, teeth being filled. Those were mantles that other ministries had that I did not have at one time.

---

[17] Luke 5:1-7

CONCLUSION

We are going to end by looking at the book of Philippians. By way of background, this letter was written by Paul to a church he birthed and had raised up. He was the apostle of the work and had raised up ministers there.

The people responded to him as partners. They connected with him and did not always have their hand out without ever releasing something back. Paul taught the church at Philippi to become a part of what God was doing by giving. They learned to bless the ministry that had blessed them.

We have to learn that when we receive something we need to turn around and bless the ministry. That is part of the laws of impartation. If you want God to keep blessing you and ministry to keep pouring into you, you have to pour something back. Paul said, "*If I give unto you that which is spiritual, it is only right that you give unto me that which is natural.*"[18]

There has to be a law of reciprocity. When the minister gives to you, bless the minister. The minister is then able to pour out even more and you continue to bless the ministry.

Paul went on to talk about muzzling the ox that treads out the corn.[19] He said that if you don't support the ministries that are ministering to you, you have muzzled the ox that treads out the corn. Treading out the corn means to bring in the harvest. The ministers will become weak spiritually and won't be able to help you bring in your harvest – your harvest of your finance, the harvest of your family, the harvest of your future or of your life. When you don't support a ministry, you weaken it spiritually so that it won't be able to help you prosper, help you be blessed, help you reach your family or help you see all the things happen that you have been believing God to do.

---

[18] 1 Corinthians 9:11
[19] 1 Timothy 5:18

Paul operated under the laws of impartation. So, he wrote the letter to the church at Philippi, covenant partners, who had given once and again to his necessity.[20] In other words, they had given over and over again.

Philippians 4:14; *"Notwithstanding ye have well done, that ye did communicate with my affliction."*

"Communicate" means they gave and helped him at his point of need.

Philippians 4:15; *"Now ye Philippians know also, that in the beginning of the gospel,*

when I departed from Macedonia, no church communicated with me as concerning giving and receiving, but ye only."

Of all the churches that Paul raised up and/or ministered to, none wanted to give to him but the church of Philippi. They are also the only church that got the promise, "*my God shall supply all your needs*." But then they were the only church that sent offerings, blessed him and helped him by backing his ministry.

Paul went on to tell them that he was not trying to get their money, profit off of them or take from them.

Philippians 4:17; *"Not because I desire a gift: but I desire fruit that may abound to your account."*

When you give, God marks it down in heaven and it goes to your account. It all stacks up as a memorial offering. Look at Acts 10, the story of Cornelius. He had been giving much, praying much and the angel of the Lord came to him saying that his prayers and giving had come up before God as a memorial. In other words, it was stacking higher and higher in front of God until God said He had to do something for him. God could not deny him.

---

[20] Philippians 4:16

Paul is saying that your giving is to bring you into a new day, to get you into a position where all of heaven will say, "W*e must bless this person*." That is what it is about. Your giving puts it to your account.

My giving is what blesses me, what causes God to move in my behalf. If you don't give to me, I will still make it and flourish because someone else will. I have had people chase me down to bless me. People have transferred money to my account when I was not preaching and had not even ministered to them, but because God had spoken to them. God has spoken to people and they mailed a check to me. I don't worry about finances but I do need to teach you the truth. You can't be blessed spiritually, financially or in any other way until you understand these principles.

The Philippians had become Paul's covenant partners. He goes on to say:

Philippians 4:18; ***"But I have all, and abound: I am full, having received of Epaphroditus the things which were sent from you, an odour of a sweet smell, a sacrifice acceptable, wellpleasing to God."***

They sacrificially gave and it smelled good to God. If you give so much that God smells it and breathes deeply, then you have done good with your offering.

Let's say you gave a fear offering. You were afraid so you didn't do what the Lord said. You have given God a smelly offering and He is not going to bless it. You would have been better off not putting anything in. What little bit you gave, you may need.

When you give a faith offering, faith smells good to God. Sacrifice smells good to God. Obedience smells good to God. When He smells it and it smells good, He will release all the blessings of heaven. Are you ready for a spiritual harvest as well as a financial harvest?

When you start getting a spiritual harvest you will experience an intimacy with God that you never experienced before. You will experience angelic visitations, visitations of Jesus, revelations at levels you never had before. There will be activations of things in the spirit realm. When God gets ready to bless you He releases more than money. Thank God for the financial, but that is nothing compared to the spiritual things He can pour on you.

The Philippians had observed Paul and watched his life. He had ministered to them, taught them, had lived his life before them.

It is important that we have covenant relationships with ministries. You need to receive more from a minister than just his words, just his teaching. You need to watch an example of life, of faith, of prayer, of dedication, of a fire for the world, of a fire for souls, a fire for healings and miracles. Then follow that example and catch the fire for those things.

Philippians 4:9; *"Those things, which ye have both <u>learned</u>, and received, and heard, and seen in me, do: and the God of peace* [wholeness, wellness] ***shall be with you."***

Even though *"peace"* in this passage is a Greek word, it is tied to the Old Testament words shalom and shalem which mean wholeness, wellness, nothing broken, nothing missing, nothing lacking.

Paul was telling the Philippians, "*You can't learn anything until someone has taught you something. The things you have learned, the things you have received, the things you have heard, the things you have seen in me now do and if you will, the God of peace will be with you. There will be nothing missing, nothing lacking. You will be complete and whole in every area, every arena.*"

Learned

"Learned" means to understand by revelation the things you have learned by revelation.

Paul spoke revelation. He didn't just teach facts, figures and certain doctrines, though doctrine was involved in it. He taught revelatory information by revelation and brought understanding to the minds of the people who heard him. We can see this best in Ephesians 3:1-5.

Ephesians 3:1-5; *"For this cause I Paul, the prisoner of Jesus Christ for you Gentiles, If ye have heard of the dispensation* [of revelation] ***of***

the grace of God which is given me to you-ward: How that by revelation he made known unto me the mystery; (as I wrote afore in few words, Whereby, when ye read, ye may understand my knowledge in the mystery of Christ) Which in other ages was not made known unto the sons of men, as it is now revealed unto his holy apostles and prophets by the Spirit;"

Paul was moving into a new dispensation, a dispensation of revelation. He was unveiling some truths to them they could understand so that they would not lack in anything.

If you are lacking in anything, it is a revelation lack. There is something you don't have the revelation on.

We need to be taught revelation. We need to have ministries who are not just giving us sermons, but who are unveiling revelation, moving in the dispensation of revelation. I would rather have a five-minute talk with revelation pouring out than forty-five minutes of just bible knowledge, of bible study.

Revelation is what changes us and brings us to manifestation. Paul said he was moving in the dispensation of revelation and the Philippians learned by revelation. You can't really learn spiritual truths unless you learn them by revelation. You need somebody who is going to preach the Word, who sits before the very feet of Jesus and lets the Spirit of God begin to come upon them. They hear the Lord speak. He is real to them and from His lips come the unfolding of Holy Scripture. They come with a message from the heart of God. There is a difference.

You can have a five point sermon or a six point sermon and I may use those but I do my best to hear from God, to hear His voice. If He is not giving it, what good is it for me to try to give it? It will bore you stiff, not feed you, not cause you to mature, not give you the victory that you need in your life.

Received

Philippians 4:9; *"Those things, which ye have both learned, and received, and heard, and seen in me, do: and the God of peace shall be with you."*

"Received" means to receive because of close relationship, to catch a tangible anointing, to catch a mantle.

So, Paul was saying that not only did they hear revelation, not only were they taught revelation but they drew near to him with their heart until they received and caught a mantle. Remember Elijah and Elisha? Elisha had to catch the mantle. When it fell, he had to see it and go after it. The only way he could do that was to be in the same area, the same arena. It had to do with close relationship.

We need to build a relationship with our trainers, with the five-fold ministry. They are to train us, to equip us to do the work of the ministry.[21] Build a relationship with them, know that they have something to impart from Jesus. They have something to give us that we don't have. Don't ever come to the place of pride where you feel like you have received it all, that you have it all. At the moment you feel like you have received as much as everybody else, you have died spiritually. That is the worst thing that can happen to you. The devil has deceived you with a religious spirit, a spirit of religious pride.

There are some ministers who have been in the ministry about nine years and they are shaking nations, having throne room experiences. I could get full of pride and say I can't learn from them because I am older than they are and have been in the ministry over thirty years. If I do that I have cut myself off spiritually and have gone as far as I can go. Humility says that somebody younger can teach me something.

We need a close intimate relationship so that we can catch the mantles. A mantle cannot be taught. It has to be caught. I can teach a revelation to you or I can teach you how to catch a mantle.

---

[21] Ephesians 4:11-12

The mantle is caught because of your diligence, because you pressed in close to a ministry, because you developed a relationship. Even when Elijah told Elisha to stay behind because he was going to go on, Elisha answered, "*As the Lord lives and as you live, I will not leave you.*"

In today's world it is very easy for people to separate themselves from a minister's life and ministry. All they have to do is say one little thing controversial and we don't want to support them anymore. What would have happened to Elisha if, when Elijah told him to stay behind, he had said, "*Okay, you don't want me around so I am out of here. Some man of God you are if you are pushing people away. I tried to serve you for twenty years and now you are treating me like this.*"

Some Christians today would have stayed behind and lost the mantle. Elijah tried to offend Elisha three times and not just once. If you can't be offended, then the devil cannot hold back anything God has for you. If you can be offended you will have nothing in God.

Psalms 119:165; *"Great peace have they which love thy law: and nothing shall offend them."*

If you really love God and love His Word, you can't be offended. Elisha didn't get offended, even though Elijah said some very offensive things to him three times. Why? Because there will be a testing as to whether or not you can handle the mantle. A lot of it has to do with being offended. If you can be easily offended then you can't handle a mantle. If you carry a mantle there will be demons saying evil stuff against you.

Every new mantle comes with great persecution. Every new mantle comes with demonic attack. If you are easily offended by people, how are you going to handle demons? You're not. So, somewhere we are going to have to get healed up enough that we can say, "*Great peace have they which love thy law and nothing shall offend them. I won't be offended and can't be offended because I love God and His Word too much.*"

Besides that, you can't offend a dead person. Maybe your flesh is too alive. You can walk up to a casket, holler, scream and tongue, but you cannot offend a corpse. The bible says we to our flesh.

Colossians 3:3; ***"For ye are dead, and your life is hid with Christ in God."***

If our flesh is dead, no one can offend us.

Heard

Philippians 4:9; ***"Those things, which ye have both learned, and received, and heard, and seen in me, do: and the God of peace shall be with you."***

"Heard" means to hear with the heart. Paul talked about the things they had heard, not with their natural ears, but with their spiritual ears.

Isaiah 50:4-5; ***"The Lord GOD hath given me the tongue of the learned*** [of the disciple]***, that I should know how to speak a word in season to him that is weary: he wakeneth morning by morning, he wakeneth mine ear to hear as the learned*** [as a disciple]***. The Lord GOD hath opened mine ear, and I was not rebellious, neither turned away back."***

This is hearing connected with the heart. You can't hear with the heart until you become a disciple, a follower of Jesus and a follower of those who are following Christ. Paul said to follow him as he follows Christ.

If people say they are following Jesus, but are not following or connecting with five-fold ministry, then they are not following Christ. God has raised up a five-fold ministry to minister to the church. Even though I move in the office of a prophet and apostle I still submit to the five-fold ministry. I have to have them. I listen to them teach and preach. Loving and supporting them, I connect with them and grow.

Jesus is the head of the body and the five-fold ministry are the trainers of the body. If you want to be in the middle of what God is doing today, you have to be in the middle of the body of Christ. You have to connect with other people, be able to learn from somebody else and know that there are other people you have to be dependent on.

Seen

Philippians 4:9; ***"Those things, which ye have both learned, and received, and heard, and seen*** [perceived] ***in me, do: and the God of peace shall be with you."***

In a precious chapter, I shared some things with you from 2 Kings 2:10-12. Elijah said to Elisha, "*Ask what I shall give you before you be taken from me.*" Elisha asked for a double portion of the Spirit of God that was upon Elijah. Elijah responded by saying he had asked a hard thing, nevertheless if Elisha saw him when he went then he would have it. Remember, *to see* means *to perceive*.

Sometimes we are so caught up in looking at the flesh, at ourselves or at the natural that we cannot perceive the gift of God in other people. If you look at me in the natural, I have nothing you can benefit from. The bible says there is no good thing in the flesh.[22]

There is something in me to be released to you that is beyond the natural realm, but you have to perceive it or you will never get it. You have to look into a ministry and see the gift of God, perceive who they really are, or you will never get it. What you don't perceive, you will never receive. If you don't perceive the gift of God, you won't receive the gift of God.

To receive a prophet in the name of the prophet means you have to perceive the prophetic gift in that person. They may be rough around the edges, may not look like anyone to you, but have the prophetic gift inside and have a lot to give. Others might be dressed flashy, preach just right, do everything just right and have nothing to give. Some may be decked out, do everything right in the natural and be right in the spirit as well. You can't look at the package and determine yea or nay. You can't look at the outside and say whether or not they have the prophetic gift. You have to perceive what is inside them.

2 Kings 2:9-11; ***"And it came to pass, when they were gone over, that Elijah said unto Elisha, Ask what I shall do for thee, before I be taken***

---

[22] Romans 7:18

away from thee. And Elisha said, I pray thee, let a double portion of thy spirit be upon me. And he said, Thou hast asked a hard thing: nevertheless, if thou see [perceive] ***me when I am taken from thee, it shall be so unto thee; but if not, it shall not be so. And it came to pass, as they still went on, and talked, that, behold, there appeared a chariot of fire, and horses of fire, and parted them both asunder; and Elijah went up by a whirlwind into heaven.***

You will get what you perceive. If you can't perceive it you can't receive it.

2 Kings 2:12; ***And Elisha saw it, and he cried, My father, my father, the chariot of Israel, and the horsemen thereof. And he saw him no more: and he took hold of his own clothes, and rent them in two pieces."***

Do you know what Elisha saw? In the Hebrew, the word *"father"* means progenitor, inheritor, and one that has something to give. You have to be able to look at a ministry and realize that it has something to give you. There is an inheritance for you inside that ministry. If you can't perceive that they have something to give you that is worth more than anything in this world, you will not get it. But if you can perceive it, you can have it all.

Do

Philippians 4:9; ***"Those things, which ye have both learned*** [by revelation]***, and received*** [because you pressed into a close relationship and caught a mantle]***, and heard*** [with your heart, not just with your natural ears]***, and seen in me*** [perceived who I really was and what I had to give to you]***, do: and the God of peace shall be with you."***

The Greek word for *"do"* is *prasso*. It means to practice, to execute, to put to practice, to do, to step into those things.

The five-fold ministries' job is not just to preach to you, lay hands on you, prophesy to you, tickle your spiritual fancy a little bit, get you excited or stirred up, but to impart what they have to you. They are to give you something you don't have yet that will change your life forever, bring you into the glory, bring you into a closer relationship, bring you into the prophetic and cause your eyes to see, your ears to hear, your five senses to perceive and receive intimate, dynamic, glorious encounters with the Lord and angelic visitations from heaven.

Then it is your job to do these things.

Made in the USA
Columbia, SC
01 July 2020

12841091R00046